Internet 2E
Office Projects

» SUSAN EVANS JENNINGS, ED. D.

Assistant Professor of General Business
Stephen F. Austin State University
Nacogdoches, TX

» SUSAN JAMES

Computer Systems Engineer
Lawrence Berkeley National Laboratory
University of California
Berkeley, CA

THOMSON
™
SOUTH-WESTERN

Australia   Canada   Mexico   Singapore   Spain   United Kingdom   United States

THOMSON

SOUTH-WESTERN

Internet Office Projects, 2E
Susan Evans Jennings and Susan James

VP/Editorial Director:
Jack W. Calhoun

VP/Editor-in-Chief:
Dave Shaut

Senior Publisher:
Karen Schmohe

Acquisitions Editor:
Joseph Vocca

Project Manager:
Dr. Inell Bolls

Production Manager:
Tricia Matthews Boies

Production Editor:
Colleen A. Farmer

Director Educational Marketing:
Carol Volz

Marketing Manager:
Mike Cloran

Manufacturing Coordinator:
Charlene Taylor

Design Project Manager:
Stacy Jenkins Shirley

Copyeditor:
Marianne Miller

Compositor:
D&G Limited, LLC

Cover Designer:
Knapke Design, Mason, OH

Internal Designer:
Knapke Design, Mason, OH

Printer:
Banta Book Group
Menasha, WI

Build Office Skills with Other Products
Available from South-Western!

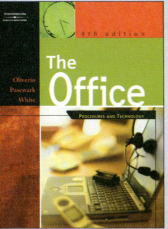

The Office: Procedures and Technology 4E
(ISBN 0-538-43475-9)

The Office is a comprehensive office-procedures text that focuses on the necessary skills for office workers. Skills covered range from using e-mail and the Internet to the use of integrated applications and Office suites. All activities are task-oriented, encouraging students to apply knowledge and skills learned to solve problems.

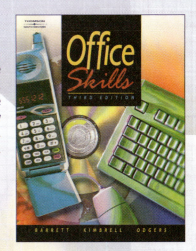

Office Skills 3E (ISBN 0-538-43485-6)

Office Skills provides up-to-date, real-life, and valuable information for survival in the office of tomorrow. The text emphasizes practical applications, everyday skills, and the knowledge needed to be successful. *Office Skills* presents an overview of technological skills and examines attitudes and human relationships, highlighting the "people skills" vital to a successful career.

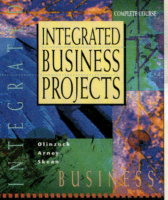

Integrated Business Projects
(ISBN 0-538-72152-9)

Integrated Business Projects is a fun but challenging, applications-oriented text that reinforces the major office applications found in suite software—word processing, electronic presentations, spreadsheets, and databases. Information about various common office careers that use these applications is included to demonstrate the real-world significance of learning the software.

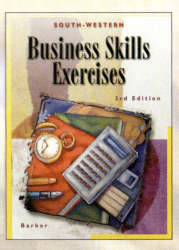

Business Skills Exercises 3E
(ISBN 0-538-69481-5)

This book provides realistic experiences in improving skills required for entry-level business employment. A combination classwork/home study approach is used. Each exercise has a stated goal so the purpose and necessity of each exercise is clear. Exercises are divided into three units, followed by a unit test to assess understanding of the information covered.

THOMSON
SOUTH-WESTERN

For more information on these and other South-Western office technology products, visit
www.swlearning.com

Preface

The Internet has changed the way offices conduct business. Administrative professionals now have at their fingertips the tools needed to make their jobs easier and more productive. In preparing these projects, we consulted office professionals from many fields to make the tasks as realistic as possible. Unlike some books that provide disks with simulated Internet addresses, these projects ask you to find actual working Internet sites. Since you will be using Net Keywords to assist in your search of a subject instead of a given site, the problem of sites no longer being in existence is not an issue.

The projects are designed to be used in a variety of settings. The tasks are geared toward real-life applications that increase your knowledge of the Internet and enhance your employability. The design of the text-workbook allows it to be used as a stand-alone Internet course, as a supplement to a computer course, or as an addition to an office procedures course, teaching Internet skills while enhancing students' understanding of a variety of office positions. Projects are designed so you can work independently with little or no instructor guidance.

»Message to the Student

Nothing is changing faster in the world today than technology. By the time you finish this text-workbook, you will have achieved a level of proficiency that allows you to confidently and effectively utilize the Internet as an indispensable tool in a variety of real applications. The ability to excel in online research can only enhance your advancement in your chosen career field. In writing this book, our goal is for you to look forward to each project as an enjoyable and entertaining way to learn.

»Features

- A project-approach uses the Internet as a research tool.
- Business scenarios offer users real workplace settings for conducting Internet research.
- Numerous Internet screen captures are used to add realism and interest.
- Net Notes, Keywords, and Surf's Up activities provide additional learning options.
- Internet research activities offered at the end of each project reinforce Internet proficiency and promote higher-order thinking skills. In addition, these activities help develop writing skills and the ability to evaluate information and draw conclusions.
- The IRCD, Instructor's Resource CD, contains an e-manual with answers and web sites for recapturing Internet URLs needed to complete activities.
- A web site for the text at *www.iop.swlearning. com* is available and contains additional Internet activities.

»Learning Aids in the Text

- Scenarios are used to add reality to the projects. These scenarios describe the position being temporarily filled.
- The projects are divided into tasks for the day. The tasks are designed to simulate the actual Internet uses for the type of office. Each task includes Net Keywords to assist with searches.
- Internet research activities are included at the end of each project. These research activities can be used as part of the regular assignment or as an enrichment exercise.

»SEARCH ENGINES

You will quickly find that search engines vary in their effectiveness. Most veteran surfers become acclimated to the differences and learn which engine is best for any given search. You can begin by going online and doing a search for the comparison of search engines. This will provide you with information about the various search engines and their features. Listed below are some of the authors' favorites. These sites are not meant to be a complete list of all search engines.

http://www.google.com
http://www.dogpile.com
http://www.infoseek.com
http://www.hotbot.com
http://www.northernlight.com
http://www.excite.com
http://www.webcrawler.com
http://www.altavista.com
http://www.lycos.com
http://www.yahoo.com

»ABOUT THE AUTHORS

Dr. Susan Evans Jennings' experience in the office technology field is extensive. Her teaching experience includes over 17 years at the high school and university levels. She is currently an Assistant Professor of General Business at Stephen F. Austin State University in Nacogdoches, Texas. Dr. Jennings' research interest is the Internet used as an educational resource and online teaching and learning tool. She has presented many workshops at the state, regional, national, and international level concerning the use of the Internet and online learning. She holds an A.A.S. in Office Occupations, a B.S.E and M.Ed. in Business Education, and an Ed.D. in Developmental Education—Instructional Systems and Technology. Her past experience in the office includes working nine years in a number of office positions for an oil company. In addition to teaching, Dr. Jennings served as business education/general cooperative education coordinator, and FBLA sponsor at Parkers Chapel High School in El Dorado, Arkansas. She was an Assistant Professor of Vocational Education at Valdosta State University in Valdosta, Georgia.

Susan James is a Computer Systems Engineer at the Lawrence Berkeley National Laboratory at the University of California, Berkeley, where she manages Unix Systems for scientists who are performing scientific research. She also builds and maintains high performance technical computers for Scientists who are doing scientific computing. Her career work includes part-time teaching in information science at various college computer labs. She holds a bachelor's degree in health science and a master's degree in public health. Her recent degrees include an A.S. in accounting, information science, and network administration. She is a Certified Novell Administrator (CNA) and a Certified Microsoft Professional (CMP). She continues to pursue her studies in computer science at the University of California, Berkeley.

»ACKNOWLEDGMENTS

I would like to express my gratitude to Susan James, who was my co-author on the first edition of this text. I offer special recognition to Steve Jennings who contributed much to the development of this second edition—he was truly the "ghost co-author" on this edition. I would like to thank our reviewers, Iris Ellis of Valdosta State University and Sue Sydow of Lyons-Decatur Northeast High School, for their helpful comments. In addition, I want to thank the project manager, Dr. Inell Bolls, for her guidance, suggestions, and encouragement in completing this project. She was absolutely indispensable in the process. We also appreciate all of the input we received from numerous business professionals who shared their expertise in developing these projects.

Contents

Project 15

Planning a Vacation   105

Project 16

Web Page Design   111

Project #1

CAREER DECISIONS AND JOB SEARCH

Scenario: You are getting ready to graduate and begin the next phase of your life. You are not entirely sure what you want to do career wise. You have considered furthering your education, but you have also considered going directly into the job market. You decide to research some of your career choices to see what, if any, advanced degrees or special training are required.

RESEARCH CAREER POSSIBILITIES

The Bureau of Labor Statistics, a division of the U.S. government, has available extensive information about all types of careers. This information is compiled in a publication entitled *Occupational Outlook Handbook* which is revised every two years. This publication is available online at http://www.bls.gov/oco/home.htm. Information includes a description of what people in an occupation do, the working conditions, the training and education needs, the earnings, and the expected job prospects in a wide range of occupations.

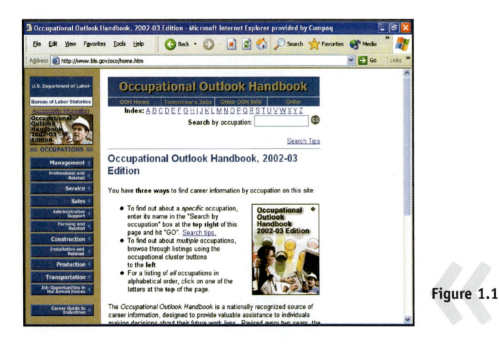

Figure 1.1

Go to the web site, and browse the categories to choose four careers you might like to pursue. Using the table on the next page, provide the information requested for those careers.

Job Title	Training Needed	Job Outlook	Median Earnings (indicate per hour or per year)
Example: Machine Transcriptionist	Post-secondary training in medical transcription preferred	Projected to grow faster than the average	$12.15 per hour (2000 information)

TASK **1-2**

RESEARCH QUALIFICATIONS AND POSITIONS AVAILABLE

While you are considering your options, you should research actual jobs currently available in your chosen profession in geographical areas in which you are interested. You need to determine the qualifications and characteristics most employers are looking for in these positions.

Figure 1.2

Many sites on the Internet provide databases of job postings. Use the Internet to find a minimum of five positions in your career interests that list desired qualifications, location of job, and salary offered.

 **Key Words:** Job Search

Job Listings

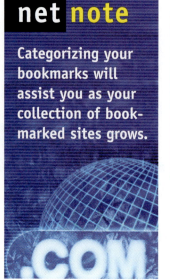

net note

Categorizing your bookmarks will assist you as your collection of book-marked sites grows.

Position	Qualifications	Job Location	Annual Salary

In these postings, what desired personal qualifications were listed most frequently?

»JOB SEARCH SITE

Internet Address: http:// _____

Description: _____

TASK 1-3

LOCATE ELECTRONIC RESUME (E-RESUME) GUIDELINES

You have decided to post an e-resume to see if you receive any interest in your qualifications for a job. It is important to know that an effective e-resume is not identical to an effective traditional resume. Locate and print out e-resume guidelines from two different sources, and answer the questions on the next page. List the web address for each source.

 Key Words: Electronic Resumes

Online Resumes

E-Resumes

Guideline Internet Addresses

http:// _____

http:// _____

What does the term *keyword* mean as it applies to an e-resume?

_____

_____

_____

_____

_____

How is the format of an e-resume different from the format of a traditional resume?

_____

_____

_____

_____

_____

Figure 1.3

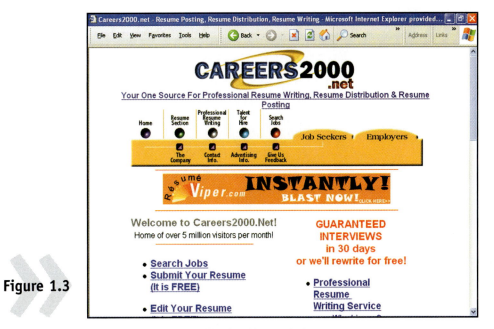

©2004 Careers2000.net. Reprinted by permission.

POST ELECTRONIC RESUMES

You have decided to use the guidelines you located to build and post an e-resume. Now you want to find three sites where you can post the e-resume. Provide the site addresses where you can build an e-resume, and answer the questions below about each site.

Key Words:	**Electronic Resume Posting**
	Online Resumes
	E-resumes

1. Is registration required for using the site to build an e-resume?
2. Do you need any special software for using the site?
3. Can you use the e-resume you build to search the site for jobs?
4. How much does it cost to post your e-resume?
5. How long will your e-resume stay posted?

Sites for Electronic Resume Posting

Site 1: http:// _____

1.	2.	3.	4.	5.

Site 2: http:// _____

1.	2.	3.	4.	5.

Site 3: http:// _____

1.	2.	3.	4.	5.

As you explore your educational and career options, you decide to seek employment with a temporary agency. This will allow you to observe various types of work environments and career areas. Using the Internet, find the names of three temporary employment agencies.

_____

_____

_____

»TEMPORARY EMPLOYMENT AGENCIES

Internet Address: http:// _____

Description: _____

Internet Research challenge:

Most people want to maximize their earning potential. They can accomplish this through specialized training, higher education, or additional experience or skills development. Using the online *Occupational Outlook Handbook* or other online sources, prepare a one- to two-page report that compares and contrasts the median annual earnings of various careers based on the educational requirements of the job (i.e., accountant, plumber, pharmacist, electrician, beautician, fire fighter, or teacher). Your report should include at least one career for each of the following: no degree, a high school degree, a technical degree, an undergraduate college degree, and an advanced college degree.

Surf's up

http://www.unitedmedia.com/comics/dilbert

http://www.espn.go.com

Project #2

THE INSURANCE OFFICE

Scenario: Today you are working as the administrative assistant to the regional sales manager, Chris Lumpkin, at Valdosta General Insurance Company in Tifton, Georgia. Mr. Lumpkin needs you to conduct some Internet research. You have been given the job of providing vital information to the sales representatives in the field so their customer calls can be more efficient and effective.

Your Internet tasks for today follow.

PREPARE LOCATION MAPS

Sales representatives for Valdosta General Insurance Company make calls to the homes of potential customers. In order to assist the representatives in planning and organizing their travel time efficiently, you are to provide them with maps showing the clients' locations. Using the addresses from the customer information request cards, use a search engine to find a site that produces location maps for the following representatives. Print copies of the maps.

Key Words:	
	Street Maps
	Map Routes
	Guide Street Maps

Representative Name: Jennifer Hicks
Territory: Lowndes County, Georgia

Valdosta General Insurance Company — Your Trusted Friend

Customer Name: Anne Adams   Phone Number: 229-862-5350
Address: 203 Sunnymeade Drive   Age: 48
Valdosta, GA 31605   Marital Status: Married
Type of Insurance Requested: Life _____   Health _____   Automobile __x__

Valdosta General Insurance Company — Your Trusted Friend

Customer Name: Glen Garcia   Phone Number: 229-862-2876
Address: 1900 Iola Drive   Age: 29
Valdosta, GA 31602   Marital Status: Single
Type of Insurance Requested: Life __x__   Health _____   Automobile _____

Representative Name: Kame Kaneshiro
Territory: Tarrant County, Texas

Valdosta General Insurance Company — Your Trusted Friend

Customer Name: Sam Wong   Phone Number: 817-222-4561
Address: 4701 Norma   Age: 76
Fort Worth, Texas 76103   Marital Status: Married
Type of Insurance Requested: Life _____   Health __x__   Automobile _____

»STREET MAPPING

Internet Address: http:// _____

_____

_____

Description: _____

_____

_____

Figure 2.1

TASK 2-2

OBTAIN TELEPHONE NUMBERS

net note

URL stands for Uniform Resource Locator. This is the address or reference code for an Internet site.

Quite often vital information is omitted from a customer information card. In this case, one card is missing the customer telephone number. Using the information available and Internet resources, locate and provide the missing information for the representatives.

Key Words:	Telephone Listings
	Telephone Directories
	Telephone Numbers
	Reverse Lookup

General Insurance Company — Your Trusted Friend

Customer Name: David Wood   Phone Number: _____

Address: Ripley Road, El Dorado, AR   Age: 53

Marital Status: Married

Type of Insurance Requested: Life __x__   Health _____   Automobile __x__

»LOCATING TELEPHONE NUMBERS

Internet Address: http:// _____

Description: _____

To track expenses at the office, employees keep a log of all long-distance calls. Occasionally a call will be made that is not listed on the log. To ascertain the recipient of the call, a reverse lookup is used. A reverse lookup provides the name of the telephone number holder based on the number, rather than the number based on the name. Determine who was called on May 21 at the following telephone number: (936) 468-3103.

Name: _____

»LOCATING TELEPHONE NUMBERS

Internet Address: http:// _____

Description: _____

TASK 2-3

DETERMINE POSTAL RATES FOR PACKAGES

Following customer meetings, representatives order company information packets from the Valdosta office (ZIP Code 31605) to be sent to potential clients. For 1-pound information packets (in a large envelope if sent U.S. mail, in a UPS letter if sent UPS, and in a FedEx® Express Pak if sent FedEx®), determine the most cost effective means of delivery among United States Mail Service, Federal Express Delivery, and United Parcel Service for second-day delivery. Record the rate in the space provided for each service. You will drop the package off at the shipper regardless of the method of shipment chosen.

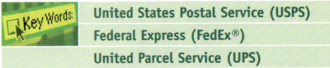

Key Words:	United States Postal Service (USPS)
	Federal Express (FedEx®)
	United Parcel Service (UPS)

Valdosta General Insurance Company — Your Trusted Friend

Customer Name: Cheri Webb Ribeiro   Phone Number: 724-660-4104

Address: 1950 N. Neshannock Rd.   Age: 45

Hermitage, PA 16148   Marital Status: Married

Type of Insurance Requested: Life _____   Health _____   Automobile ___x___

2nd Day

USPS rate: _____   FedEx rate: _____   UPS rate: _____

Valdosta General Insurance Company — Your Trusted Friend

Customer Name: Kathy Harrell   Phone Number: 918-223-4567

Address: 111 Cherry Street   Age: 42

Poteau, OK 74953   Marital Status: Single

Type of Insurance Requested: Life __x__   Health _____   Automobile __x__

2nd Day

USPS rate: _____   FedEx rate: _____   UPS rate: _____

Valdosta General Insurance Company — Your Trusted Friend

Customer Name: Juan Gonzalez   Phone Number: 417-656-7724

Address: 200 Main Street   Age: 29

Branson, MO 65616   Marital Status: Single

Type of Insurance Requested: Life __x__   Health _____   Automobile _____

2nd Day

USPS rate: _____   FedEx rate: _____   UPS rate: _____

»POSTAL/SHIPPING RATES

Internet Address: http:// _____

Description: _____

Figure 2.2

When preparing the mailing packets, you notice some information cards do not include ZIP Codes. Using the Internet, find the correct ZIP Code + 4 for the addresses listed below:

 ZIP Codes

228 Oak Avenue, Sulphur Springs, TX _____

9224 Hillman Way Drive, Memphis, TN _____

Your Address ZIP Code + 4 _____

»POSTAL ZIP CODES

Internet Address: http:// _____

Description: _____

Figure 2.3

Valdosta General prides itself on providing low-cost insurance coverage to customers. Some insurance companies now offer online quotes. Valdosta General is beginning to think about providing this service. Mr. Lumpkin would like for you to locate an online insurance company that provides online quotes and to try out this online service.

Compare the insurance rates for a 23-year-old and a 30-year-old male who each own a 2001 four-door Mitsubishi Montero Sport LS with a $500 deductible. The vehicle was purchased new in January 2001, and the average number of miles driven per year is 12,000. When answering the questions, you may require some or all of the following information. Both men were born on July 4 (you may need to provide the year of birth). If you need to supply a state or an address, use your own or choose another one. You do need to use the same state and/or address for each quote. The insurer for the past five years has been State Farm Mutual. The current policies expire one month from today. The current premium is $1,300 a year. The current policy has bodily injury limits of $50,000/$100,000. Comprehensive and collision coverage are desired. The vehicle is not used for business and it is not financed. The drivers have no accidents, claims, or tickets in the last five years. They received their driver's licenses at age 16.

Using the chart below, fill in the information requested.

$500 deductible	23-year-old male – 1-year premium	30-year-old male – 1-year premium
Company Name		

»INSURANCE INFORMATION

Internet Address: http:// _____

Description: _____

▶ PREPARE HIGHWAY MAP

The regional sales manager, Chris Lumpkin, needs to travel to the new office open-
ing in Marshall, Texas. He plans to make it a cross-country drive. Prepare a driving
map with directions from 100 N. Ashley in Valdosta, Georgia, ZIP 31601, to the
new office at 900 Jasper Drive, Marshall, Texas, ZIP 75672. You may be able to use
the same Internet site you used for Task 2-1. This time you will need to include
directions. Print the map and directions.

» HIGHWAY MAPPING

Internet Address: http:// _____

Description: _____

Internet Research challenge:

There are many types of insurance. One type is flood insurance. Using the Internet, research flood insurance. Prepare a one- to two-page report that describes flood insurance. Explain who needs flood insurance, describe the types of losses the insurance protects against, and whether those who have homeowner's insurance also need flood insurance.

Surf's up

http://www.tv-now.com/

http://www.anywho.com

(Hint: Click on the street name to get a listing of everyone who lives on your street.)

Project #3

THE EDUCATION OFFICE

Scenario: Today's position takes you to the office of Sonya Feemster, manager of a counseling and career center. Much of the information Mrs. Feemster needs to counsel clients can be found on the Internet.

The following tasks are those you need to complete today.

FIND PROFESSIONAL CERTIFICATION REQUIREMENTS

Many states require certified teachers to pass a national standardized test called the Praxis. Linda Shock holds a valid Arkansas teaching license for business education. She decides that she also wants to become certified in Guidance Counseling. She has completed the coursework but would like to know if Arkansas requires Praxis tests for adding an area of certification.

 Key Words:

Praxis Test

Educational Testing Service

What is the requirement for educators holding a valid Arkansas teaching license who wish to qualify for additional areas of licensure? _____

_____

After you provide Ms. Shock with this information, she wants to know the minimum qualifying score for initial licensure on the School Guidance & Counseling Praxis test in Arkansas. This test is in the licensure area of Guidance/Counseling. What is the minimum qualifying score? _____

In order for Ms. Shock to receive any additional information, you will also want to provide her with the telephone number for the licensing agency in the state of Arkansas. The telephone number is _____

net note

Megahertz (MHz) measure the speed of a computer's central processing unit (CPU). One megahertz is equal to 1 million cycles per second.

.COM

Figure 3.1

SAU Home Page - Microsoft Internet Explorer provided by Compaq

File   Edit   View   Favorites   Tools   »   ← Back   »   Address   http://www.saumag.edu   → Go   Links   »

SOUTHERN ARKANSAS UNIVERSITY
A Tradition of Success

DIRECTORY
CAMPUS MAP
CONTACT US
CALENDAR

about us
academics
administration
alumni
athletics
foundation
library
services

***

Links for
Visitors
Current students
Prospective students
Parents and family
Faculty and staff
Continuing Education

Today's news
SAU Plans Holiday Celebration
More SAU news......

On campus
Current Construction
SAU graduate returns for art exhibition
SAU to present workshop on teaching art, music
Listen to Mulerider football

Sarah Langley (right) helps local fourth-grader Hannah Trout with an experiment using light as part of the Science Class for Kids, sponsored by the Early Childhood Program at SAU. More . . .
SOUTHERN ARKANSAS UNIVERSITY
A Tradition of Success
Questions about the web site should be sent to
ckyoung@saumag.edu.
Southern Arkansas University
100 E. University, Magnolia, AR, 71753-5000
(870) 235-4000

start   Windows Messenger   Project 3 FINAL - Micr...   SAU Home Page - Mic...   5:32 PM

Mrs. Feemster is preparing an article on the minimum Praxis II scores required for Family & Consumer Sciences (known as Home Economics in some states) and Business Education in the states listed below. Due to a shortage of teachers in these subjects across the United States, she wants to help promote interest in teaching in these areas. Since you are already at the site for gathering this information, she asks that you fill in the chart below for her research.

State	Home Economics/ Family & Consumer Sciences	Business Education
	REQUIRED SCORES	
	Test No. 10120	Test No. 10100
Arkansas	_____	_____
Connecticut	_____	_____
Georgia	_____	_____
Hawaii	_____	_____
Indiana	_____	_____
Kentucky	_____	_____
Mississippi	_____	_____
Your State (if available)	_____	_____

Which of these states has the highest score requirement for

Home Economics/Family & Consumer Sciences? _____

for Business Education? _____

Which of these states has the lowest score requirement for

Home Economics/Family & Consumer Sciences _____

for Business Education? _____

»PRAXIS TEST INFORMATION

Internet Address: http:// _____

Description: _____

Key Words:	**Educational Testing Service**
	ACT
	SAT

Many times people call or come to Mrs. Feemster's office to obtain dates, locations, and miscellaneous information about standardized tests. Today you have the following requests:

1. Stephen Martin wants to take the ACT exam which is required for admission to many colleges and universities. He wants to know the next national test date for taking the ACT. You will need to find this information based on the next test date for which the registration deadline has not yet passed.

ACT Test Date: _____

Registration deadline for above test date: _____

Stephen also wants to know when he can expect to receive his ACT test score. Check the web site and record this information. _____

_____

2. Stephen is interested in attending a college outside the state of Arkansas. He is currently considering a program at Stephen F. Austin State University in Nacogdoches, Texas. He has been told that he is required to take a test called the TASP test in order to attend a Texas university unless he meets one of the exemption provisions. Provide Stephen with answers to the following questions.

What does TASP stand for in the Texas-based test? _____

_____

List the provisions for exemption from the TASP test.

_____

_____

_____

_____

3. Amanda Meadors, a senior at Parkers Chapel High School, wants to increase her chances of receiving a college scholarship by taking both the SAT test and the ACT test. She wants to know what the next national test date is for taking the SAT I. You need to find this information based on the next test date for which the registration deadline has not yet passed.

Test date: _____

Registration deadline for above test date: _____

Amanda wants to know how long after taking the test she can anticipate receiving her SAT test score report by mail and how she can receive the results faster.

Time required for mailed results: _____

Alternative method for receiving results: _____

Additional cost and time frame for alternative method of results: _____

_____

_____

»College Admission Test Information

Internet Address: http:// _____

Description: _____

Figure 3.2

OBTAIN INFORMATION ON GOVERNMENT FINANCIAL AID FOR STUDENTS

Mrs. Feemster is very conscientious about having students apply for any government financial aid for which they qualify.

Key Words:	FAFSA
	Financial Aid
	Government Student Aid

What is the Internet address for the home page of the Free Application for Federal Student Aid (FAFSA) program?

_____

A student, Toni Zomora, comes to ask about the major difference between a Federal Pell Grant and a Stafford Loan. Describe the difference below.

_____

_____

»FINANCIAL AID INFORMATION

Internet Address: http:// _____

Description: _____

OBTAIN SPECIFIC INFORMATION FROM COLLEGES AND UNIVERSITIES

Mrs. Feemster's office also tries to assist individuals who have specific questions about various colleges and universities in which they are interested. She receives four requests today. Use the Internet to answer the following questions.

The first request comes from Brooke Sutherlin. She wants to attend Valdosta State University in the fall. What are the minimum freshman admission requirements regarding SAT scores?

Verbal _____   Math _____

What is the application fee for applying to Valdosta State? _____

Your second visitor is Ryan Herring. In the fall, he plans to attend Stephen F. Austin State University in Nacogdoches, Texas. He wants to know which is the largest resident hall that accepts men and how many students it holds. _____

_____

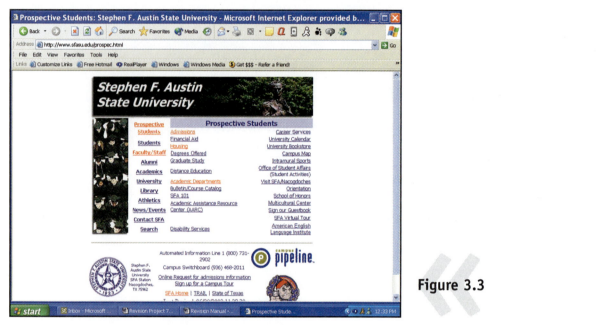

Figure 3.3

Your third visitor today is Blake Krisp. Blake is interested in attending Rice University in Houston. He wants to know the undergraduate enrollment for Rice. (Provide the most recent number available.) _____

Jenna Perdue wants to know in which building the Enrollment Services Office is located on the campus of College of the Redwoods in Eureka, California, so she can tour the campus on her approaching visit. Also provide Jenna with the local and toll-free telephone numbers for the office.

_____

_____

»University Information

Internet Address: http:// _____

Internet Address: http:// _____

Internet Address: http:// _____

Description: _____

Students are often in need of financial scholarships. With the endless number of scholarships available based on certain criteria, certain Internet sites can help you successfully navigate the possibilities. Using one of the sites listed below (or one of your own, if you prefer), find scholarship information for yourself. Since these sites require that you log in, you will need to use your own name and address. Using your own personal information, print out pages showing five scholarships for which you are eligible to apply. The printout should include the name, amount, and qualifications required for receiving the scholarship.

»INTERNET SITES

The three sites are as follows:

MACH25 – **http://www.collegenet.com/mach25**

FastWeb – **http://www.fastweb.com**

Paying for College – **http://www.collegeboard.com**

net note

The Internet is the fastest-growing media ever—faster than radio or television.

.COM

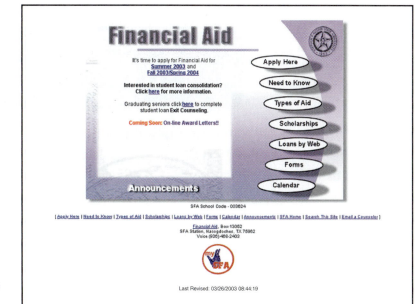

Figure 3.4

©2003 Stephen F. Austin State University. Reprinted by permission.

Internet Research challenge:

Many students make inquiries about the ACT and SAT college entrance tests. Mrs. Feemster would like to prepare a flyer that compares and contrasts these two tests. Provide information about the maximum possible scores and the major subject areas tested by each. Prepare a one- to two-page report on this topic.

http://www.foxsports.com

http://www.lavamind.com/pet_menu.html

Project #4

THE MEDICAL OFFICE

Scenario: Dr. Leah Evans is a family practitioner. Your assignment today is to fill in for her administrative assistant. Though Dr. Evans receives many professional journals and attends many conferences to stay abreast of developments in medicine, the Internet offers many resources for those in the medical profession as well as for the general public. Today, Dr. Evans puts you in charge of locating various types of information for her and her patients.

❯ TASKS

▶ **4-1**
LOCATE MEDICAL INFORMATION ON ANTHRAX

▶ **4-2**
LOCATE ADULT IMMUNIZATION SCHEDULE

▶ **4-3**
LOCATE CORPORATE HEADQUARTERS FOR HEALTH INSURANCE PROVIDER

▶ **4-4**
LOCATE PRESCRIPTION DRUG INFORMATION

▶ **4-5**
LOCATE PHYSICIANS

TASK 4-1

LOCATE MEDICAL INFORMATION ON ANTHRAX

Anthrax is a disease often associated with cattle. However, anthrax can be contracted by humans. Several of Dr. Evans' patients have expressed concern about anthrax. Dr. Evans has asked you to prepare answers to the following questions so the information can be made available to patients.

Key Words:
Healthfinder
Anthrax
Health Resources

Anthrax Information

1. What is the medical definition of the disease anthrax?

_____

_____

_____

2. What are the three major types of anthrax? Which is most common?

_____

_____

_____

Most Common: _____

3. Is anthrax generally considered to be contagious?

_____

»ANTHRAX

Internet Address: http:// _____

Description: _____

LOCATE ADULT IMMUNIZATION SCHEDULE

One of Dr. Evans' patients, Julie Kimble, has asked for a schedule of adult immunizations. Dr. Evans would like you to go to the web site of the Centers for Disease Control and Prevention to locate and print a copy of the *Summary of Adolescent/ Adult Immunization Recommendation* to send to Ms. Kimble.

 **Key Words:** Center for Disease Control

National Immunization Program

»CENTERS FOR DISEASE CONTROL

Internet Address: http:// _____

Description: _____

LOCATE CORPORATE HEADQUARTERS FOR HEALTH INSURANCE PROVIDER

A problem has come up with an unusual claim submitted to the regional office of The Prudential Insurance Company of America for one of Dr. Evans' patients, Shannon Gesford. You need to contact corporate headquarters for clarification of the procedure to be followed concerning this special circumstance. Find the address of the corporate headquarters.

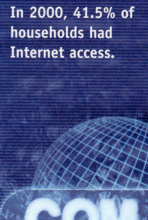

net note

In 2000, 41.5% of households had Internet access.

Key Words: Prudential

Insurance Companies on the Internet

Health Insurance

Insurance Providers

Mailing Address: _____

_____

_____

_____

»LOCATING HEALTH INSURANCE PROVIDERS

Internet Address: http:// _____

Description: _____

TASK **4-4**

LOCATE PRESCRIPTION DRUG INFORMATION

One of Dr. Evans' patients, Sarah Head, has been suffering from anxiety. Dr. Evans has prescribed the prescription drug Buspar® for the patient. She would like you to go to the manufacturer's web site for this medication, and list four common side effects of the drug.

Key Words: **Buspar**

Anti-anxiety Medication

1. _____

2. _____

3. _____

4. _____

»ANTI-ANXIETY MEDICINE

Internet Address: http:// _____

Description: _____

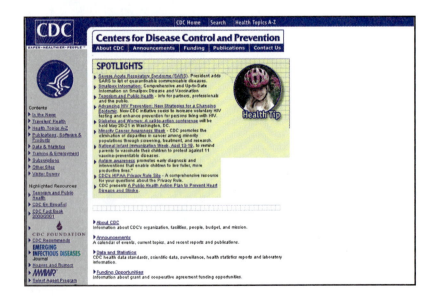

Preston Amend, one of Dr. Evans' patients, is moving to Salem, Oregon. He needs the name of a doctor in Salem who specializes in endocrinology, diabetes, and metabolism who can treat his diabetes. Use the American Medical Association listing of physicians to recommend doctors for Mr. Amend.

 American Medical Association

How many physicians were found in the search? _____

List their names below.

_____

_____

_____

_____

»AMERICAN MEDICAL ASSOCIATION

Internet Address: http:// _____

Description: _____

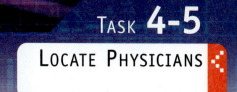

net note

It is estimated that as many as 50 million people use the Internet on a regular basis.

Internet Research challenge:

Hypertension, commonly known as high blood pressure, is often referred to as the "silent killer." Use the Internet to find information and write a one- to two-page report on the causes, effects, and preventive measures of hypertension. List three sites used in preparing the report.

Surf's up

http://www.ucomics.com/cathy/

http://www.whitehouse.gov

Project # 5

THE ACCOUNTING OFFICE

Scenario: CPA Mateo Estrada has hired you to assist in Internet research. The purpose of the research is to find information that is vital to maintaining accurate records and that Mr. Estrada needs to help his clients.

Your Internet tasks for today follow.

LOCATE DEPARTMENT OF LABOR REGULATIONS

net note

You can add frequently used e-mail addresses to your bookmark or favorites list. After entering an address as a bookmark, open the bookmark or favorites list and select the e-mail address, which automatically opens the Send Mail dialog box. The address of the recipient is added automatically.

.COM

One of your clients, Wanda Samson, wants to add her next-door neighbor, 14-year-old Jessica Mote, to her payroll. Jessica plans to work after school and on weekends in Ms. Samson's card shop. Ms. Samson wants to know what the federal laws are regarding employment of children 14 years of age. Research the answers to her questions below.

 Key Words

U. S. Department of Labor	
Child Labor Laws	

How many hours can Jessica work on school days? _____

How many hours can Jessica work on a non-school day? _____

What are the legal restrictions to the hours of the day Jessica can work?

_____

_____

»DEPARTMENT OF LABOR

Internet Address: http:// _____

Description: _____

Figure 5.1

One of Mr. Estrada's clients, Keaton Grubbs, operates a temporary employment service in Eureka, California. Mr. Grubbs needs enough employees on hand to meet demand, so he wants to find out which month(s) of the previous 12 months had the lowest national unemployment rate. Find this information on the Internet.

Key Words:	Bureau of Labor Statistics
	Economy
	Unemployment

Which of the previous 12 months had the lowest unemployment rate?

_____

»UNEMPLOYMENT RATES

Internet Address: http:// _____

Description: _____

Some of Mr. Grubbs' customers are small business owners who are unfamiliar with details of overtime pay requirements. He asks Mr. Estrada to provide him with a copy of the applicable regulations concerning the payment of overtime. Mr. Estrada determines that the regulation in question is 778.101—The Maximum Hours Provision. Locate the web site for the Department of Labor, and use their internal search feature to locate regulation 778.101. Print a copy.

| Key Words: | Department of Labor (Search Index) |
| | Overtime Regulations |

net note

According to the 2000 U.S. Census, nearly 1 in 5 people used Internet connections to check on the news, weather, and/or sports.

.COM

»LOCATING WAGE INFORMATION

Internet Address: http:// _____

Description: _____

29CFR778 - Overtime Compensation - Microsoft Internet Explorer provided by Compaq

File   Edit   View   Favorites   Tools   Help

Back   •   ⊗ ⊗ ⌂   Search   Favorites   Media   ⊗   ⊗ • ⊗   ⊠ • ☐   Address   Links

U.S. Department of Labor
in the **21st Century**

www.dol.gov   Search / A-Z Index

By Topic | By Audience | By Top 20 Requested Items | By Form | By Organization | By Location

◁ Prev   Content Last Revised: 1/26/68   Next ▷
                    ---DISCLAIMER---

CFR Code of Federal Regulations Pertaining to ESA
└ Title 29 Labor
  └ Chapter V Wage and Hour Division, Department of Labor
    └ Part 778 Overtime Compensation

Subpart Name
A   General Considerations
B   The Overtime Pay Requirements
C   Payments That May Be Excluded From the ``Regular Rate''
D   Special Problems
E   Exceptions From the Regular Rate Principles
F   Pay Plans Which Circumvent the Act
G   Miscellaneous

Authority: 52 Stat. 1060, as amended: 29 U.S.C. 201 et seq.

Figure 5.2

Task **5-4**

DETERMINE PROPER MAILING ADDRESS FOR TAX FILING

Mr. Estrada has a client, Olatunde Ogunyemi, who moved to Amherst, Massachusetts. Mr. Estrada completed his client's federal tax return but does not have the pre-printed envelope to send in the return. Go to the web site of the Internal Revenue Service, and find the correct mailing address for Mr. Ogunyemi's federal tax return.

 Key Words: **Internal Revenue Service**

Mailing Address: _____

_____

_____

_____

»INTERNAL REVENUE SERVICE

Internet Address: http:// _____

Description: _____

Figure 5.3

GATHER STATE INCOME TAX INFORMATION

One of Mr. Estrada's clients, Beverly Oswalt, is planning to retire and would like to move to a state that has no state income tax. Mr. Estrada asks you for a list of states that meet this criterion. He also asks you to note the lowest maximum rate, and the highest maximum rate for the states with income taxes.

 State Income Tax Rates

States with no income taxes:

_____

_____

Lowest maximum rate: _____

Highest maximum rate: _____

»STATE INCOME TAX

Internet Address: http:// _____

Description: _____

net note

You will find a wide range of difference between hits on various search engines even when given identical search criteria. You need to experiment to find the search engines that provide the information you desire.

FIND CPA EXAM AND TEST DATE INFORMATION

Mr. Estrada has been asked to speak at his college alma mater on the subject of certified public accountancy. The committee in charge of planning has asked that he provide information about the day-to-day activities of CPA work as well as the requirements to become a CPA. Mr. Estrada asks you to use the Internet to research the formal name of each of the four parts of the CPA exam. He would like you to print out a schedule of upcoming test dates to hand out to the students. He would also like the names of three companies that offer educational programs for reviewing for the CPA exam.

Key Words:	
	CPA Test
	CPA Test Date
	CPA Test Review

The four parts of the CPA exam:

_____

_____

_____

_____

Three companies that offer review courses:

_____

_____

_____

»CPA EXAM

Internet Address: http:// _____

Description: _____

Internet Research challenge:

As the chair of the Ethics Committee of the state CPA professional organization, Mr. Estrada is very interested in the ethical practices of CPAs and the image they project to the public. He would like to prepare a report on ethical accounting practices to share with his fellow members. In preparation for this report, he would like you to compose a one- to two-page report on the accounting firm that was under federal scrutiny in the 2001–2002 Enron Corporation controversy. Your report should include the name of the accounting firm, the charges the firm faced, the firm's questionable practices and the incidents leading up to the charges, and the current status of the accounting firm.

http://www.kissthisguy.com

http://www.imagestation.com

Project #6

THE LEGAL OFFICE

Scenario: You work as a legal research assistant for the law firm of Ellis, Sutherlin, and Perez located in Montgomery, Alabama. You are asked to locate information using online resources.

The following are the Internet tasks you need to complete today.

LOCATE EXPERT WITNESSES

Iris Ellis, a law partner, is handling an accident case for Charles Backes. Mr. Backes was involved in an accident at a local amusement park. Ms. Ellis and Mr. Backes believe the park was negligent in its maintenance of the rides. To strengthen their case, Ms. Ellis wants to bring in an expert witness on amusement parks. This person would be an expert who determines if rides such as ferris wheels, roller coasters, and bumper cars were properly designed, maintained, operated, and supervised. Locate the names and telephone numbers of two possible expert witnesses for Ms. Ellis.

Expert Court Witness

Legal Expert Witnesses

ExpertPages

»EXPERT WITNESS INFORMATION

Internet Address: http:// _____

Description: _____

Figure 6.1

LOCATE THE NAMES OF ELECTED OFFICIALS

Mr. Matthew Sutherlin, a law partner, was recently elected president of the western region of the American Bar Association. All members' state governors are invited to attend the regional conference. Obtain the name of the governor for each of the states in the western region.

Key Words:	(State) Government Directories
	State Governors

California _____

Oregon _____

Washington _____

Idaho _____

Arizona _____

Nevada _____

»STATE GOVERNOR INFORMATION

Internet Address: http:// _____

Description: _____

LOCATE U.S. COURT OF APPEALS DISTRICTS

Pilar Perez's client, Amy Counts, is a resident of Massachusetts and is unsatisfied with the lower court ruling in her legal case. She wants her case presented before the U.S. Court of Appeals. Determine in which U.S. Court of Appeals Circuit District Ms. Perez needs to file Ms. Counts' case.

net **note**

The dominant age group of Internet users is 13–35. The average age is 31.

Key Words:

Federal Courts Finder

United States Court of Appeal

United States Government

United States Judicial System

Circuit District # _____

»U.S. COURT OF APPEALS

Internet Address: http:// _____

Description: _____

Figure 6.2

▶ OBTAIN INFORMATION ON FEDERAL AGENCIES

Ms. Ellis' clients, Vicki and Bob McGowan, have a case involving an oil spill on the property they own in Kerens, Texas. Ms. Ellis needs to contact the Environmental Protection Agency's regional office to determine what action the firm should take regarding the spill. Your job is to locate the region that has jurisdiction and to obtain the mailing address.

 Key Words:

EPA Districts

Federal Agencies

Environmental Protection Agency

Region # _____

Mailing Address: _____

_____

_____

»EPA INFORMATION

Internet Address: http:// _____

Description: _____

Mr. Lloyd Evans, a client of Ms. Ellis, has asked that she provide him with answers to the questions below regarding citizenship in the United States. Mr. Evans has resided in the United States legally for four years.

Key Words: **United States Immigration**

US Immigration and Naturalization

What is the required length of legal residence before citizenship may be requested?

_____

What is the legal age requirement for citizenship? _____

Mr. Evans would also like a copy of the Oath of Allegiance. Print a copy.

»CITIZENSHIP INFORMATION

Internet Address: http:// _____

Description: _____

Figure »» **6.3**

▶ RESEARCH MINIMUM WAGE LAWS

net note

The average Internet surfer spends approximately 5 ½ hours on the Internet each week.

Ms. Perez intends to give a speech to the Rotary Club regarding the economic effects of the Minimum Wage Law on commerce. She asks you to find the effective dates and wage amounts for the three minimum wage increases that occurred after 1990. This information is compiled monthly by the Bureau of Labor Statistics.

 Key Words:

| U.S. Department of Labor |
| Minimum Wage Laws |

_____

_____

_____

Ms. Perez needs a visual aid for her Rotary presentation. She would like a chart or graph showing the changes in the minimum wage since it began—one in absolute dollars or one that reflects the impact of inflation. Print out the chart or graph.

»MINIMUM WAGE INFORMATION

Internet Address: http:// _____

Description: _____

Internet Research challenge:

Mr. Sutherlin will be presenting a workshop on bankruptcy options. He would like you to prepare a one- to two-page report on the subject. In this report, provide information about the differences between a Chapter 7 and a Chapter 13 bankruptcy.

Surf's up

http://www.bluemountain.com

http://www.hallmarkconnections.com

Project #7

PREVIEW

The Radio Station

Scenario: The content coordinator for local radio station WKLA in Cincinnati, Ohio, is leaving on vacation. You have been hired to fill in. Much of the work you will be performing involves finding information that can be used for between-music fillers, contests, news, and weather. You will rely heavily on the Internet for many of these tasks.

Following is the information needed for today's taping.

Find the three-day weather forecast for Cincinnati, and fill in the information below.

"Looking ahead at this week's weather we find . . . ." In the first blank, provide the condition (for example, clear, cloudy, rainy, or stormy). In the second blank, provide the predicted high and low.

net note

All Fortune 500 companies have a web site or are designing one.

 Key Words: **Weather**

Weather Forecasts

	Condition	High/Low Temperature
Today:	_____	_____
Day 2:	_____	_____
Day 3:	_____	_____

»WEATHER INFORMATION

Internet Address: http:// _____

Description: _____

Figure 7.1

LOCATE CURRENT MOVIE REVIEWS

Each day the DJ, Maria Aguilar, provides a movie review during her entertainment segment. Find reviews for three current movies. These movie reviews can be from any Internet source, but list the source so the DJ can give on-air credit to the reviewer. List the movies you choose, and print out the reviews.

Key Words:	Movie Reviews
	Film Critiques
	Movie Choices

Movie 1/Reviewer: _____

Movie 2/Reviewer: _____

Movie 3/Reviewer: _____

»MOVIE REVIEWS

Internet Address: http:// _____

Description: _____

LOCATE EVENTS HAPPENING ON THIS DAY IN HISTORY

The late-night DJ, S. K. (So Kool) Jennings, is a history buff. On his "Blast from the Past" segment, he likes to provide listeners with information about historical or interesting events that happened in years past on today's date. For his program tonight, list three events that occurred on today's date. These do not have to be particularly significant events—just interesting.

Key Words:
Historical Events Date
Historical Trivia

net note

In a 1998 study, eighty-two percent of web users considered web access to be "indispensable."

Event 1: _____

Event 2: _____

Event 3: _____

»HISTORICAL EVENTS

Internet Address: http:// _____

Description: _____

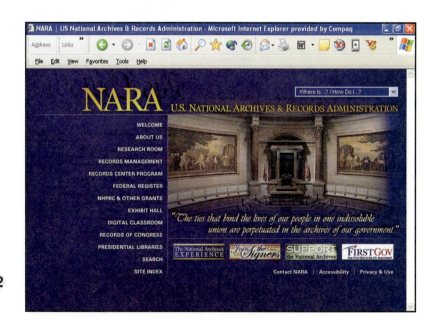

Figure 7.2

During the morning show before the birthday giveaway, the DJ announces famous birthdays. Find two famous birthdays for today's date.

 Famous Birthdays

Historical Trivia

Birthday 1: _____

Birthday 2: _____

While you are at this site, look up the names of two famous people who share your birthday.

What is your birthday? _____

List two famous people with this same birthday.

_____

_____

»FAMOUS BIRTHDAYS

Internet Address: http:// _____

Description: _____

FIND HOROSCOPE FOR TODAY'S BIRTHDAY

During the birthday segment, the DJ also reads the horoscope for today's birthday celebrators. Find the horoscope for those born today.

Key Words:	**Horoscope**
	Astrology

Print out the page with the horoscope listed. If more than one is listed per page, circle the correct horoscope for today's date.

»HOROSCOPE

Internet Address: http:// _____

Description: _____

net note

There are over 50 million web pages. This means you can find information on practically anything online. However, it does require skill (and sometimes luck) to find it.

.COM

Internet Research challenge:

A local movie rental store is sponsoring a trivia contest. Each month a different movie is showcased for trivia questions. The name of the first caller with the correct answer goes into a drawing. At the end of the month, a name is drawn. The winner receives 25 free movie rentals. Next month's movie is *Gone With the Wind*. Using the Internet, prepare a list of 31 trivia questions (one for each day of the month) and their answers to be used on the show. Topics may include: actors, actresses, awards, settings, famous quotes, etc.

http://www.rockhall.com

http://www.cg.tuwien.ac.at/~helwig/smileys.html

Project #8

FINANCIAL INVESTMENT OFFICE

Scenario: As the temporary administrative assistant at Megabucks Investments for financial adviser Jeane Owens, you are requested to perform online research to find information about investment opportunities for clients.

Your Internet tasks for the day follow.

⟩ TASKS

▶ **8-1**
OBTAIN STOCK SYMBOLS

▶ **8-2**
OBTAIN STOCK NAMES

▶ **8-3**
OBTAIN STOCK PRICES

▶ **8-4**
OBTAIN PRICE/EARNINGS (P/E) RATIO

▶ **8-5**
OBTAIN MUTUAL FUND PRICES

▶ **8-6**
OBTAIN STOCK PRICE TRENDS

TASK 8-1

OBTAIN STOCK SYMBOLS

net note

One thousand gigabytes is called a terabyte.

Mrs. Diane Howard, one of the firm's clients, has an interest in purchasing stock from the following companies. Find the stock symbol for each of the companies listed below.

Key Words:	
	Stockfind
	PCQuote
	NASDAQ
	American Stock Exchange (amex)
	New York Stock Exchange
	Microsoft Investor (Research Center)

Sears Roebuck & Co. _____

Eastman Kodak _____

BellSouth _____

»STOCK SYMBOLS

Internet Address: http:// _____

Description: _____

One of Ms. Owens' clients, John Gross, received his most current stock statement. He finds that he has forgotten the actual names of some of the stocks. He would like you to provide the names for him. Given the list of stock symbols below, find the full name of each company.

Key Words:
- **NASDAQ**
- **Stockfind**
- **PCQuote**
- **American Stock Exchange (amex)**
- **New York Stock Exchange**
- **Microsoft Investor (Research Center)**

New York Stock Exchange

A _____   KO _____

BA _____   Z _____

American Stock Exchange

DVN _____   NBR _____

NASDAQ

CHS _____   IDTI _____

MSFT _____   CSCO _____

»STOCK NAMES

Internet Address: http:// _____

Description: _____

OBTAIN STOCK PRICES

net note

The term *cyberspace* was originated by author William Gibson in his novel *Neuromancer.*

One of your calls this morning was from a client, Ms. Rebecca Sosa, who would like to know today's price on some of her stocks that she is considering selling. Using the Internet, find the current price for the stocks listed below:

> **Key Words:**
>
> **NASDAQ**
> **American Stock Exchange (amex)**
> **New York Stock Exchange**
> **Microsoft Investor (Research Center)**
> **Stockfind**
> **PCQuote**

Stock Name	Stock Symbol	Today's Price
WalMart	_____	_____
Coinstar	_____	_____
Petsmart	_____	_____
Southwest Airlines	_____	_____

»OBTAINING STOCK PRICES

Internet Address: http:// _____

_____

Description: _____

_____

_____

OBTAIN PRICE/EARNINGS (P/E) RATIO

The P/E ratio is a basic evaluation for stocks. It is generally provided on sites that contain stock performance data. Ms. Owens needs a list of the Price to Earnings ratio for the stocks below, as many of her conservative clients will only buy stocks with low P/E ratios.

Key Words:	Microsoft Investor (Research Center)
	Stockfind
	PCQuote

KR	_____	EFII	_____
GM	_____	JBLU	_____

»PRICE/EARNINGS (P/E) RATIO

Internet Address: http:// _____

Description: _____

OBTAIN MUTUAL FUND PRICES

Some of Mrs. Owens' clients want to invest in the stock market but do not feel they have the time or experience needed to pick individual stocks. These people may invest in mutual funds, which are professionally managed groups of stocks. Find the symbols for the following popular mutual funds and their current prices. Mutual funds generally have five-letter symbols. The prices may be given as NAV (net asset value) which do not reflect any sales commissions.

 Microsoft Investor (Research Center)
Mutual Funds

Fund Name	Symbol	Current Price (NAV)
Fidelity Magellan	_____	_____
Putnam Voyager A	_____	_____
American Funds New Economy A	_____	_____

»MUTUAL FUNDS

Internet Address: http:// _____

Description: _____

OBTAIN STOCK PRICE TRENDS

Investors may want to study stock price trends. A stock price trend simply means the price variations over a given time period. Use the Internet to find the 52-week high and 52-week low for each of the stocks on the next page. Determine whether the stock is currently trading nearer its high or low for the past year.

Key Words:

- Microsoft Investor (Research Center)
- Stockfind
- PCQuote

Stock: General Motors Stock Symbol: ____________

52-Week High: ____________ 52-Week Low: ____________

This stock is currently trading nearer the: High Low (circle one)

Stock: Ford Motor Stock Symbol: ____________

52-Week High: ____________ 52-Week Low: ____________

This stock is currently trading nearer the: High Low (circle one)

Stock: IBM Stock Symbol: ____________

52-Week High: ____________ 52-Week Low: ____________

This stock is currently trading nearer the: High Low (circle one)

Stock: Ryanair Holdings Stock Symbol: ____________

52-Week High: ____________ 52-Week Low: ____________

This stock is currently trading nearer the: High Low (circle one)

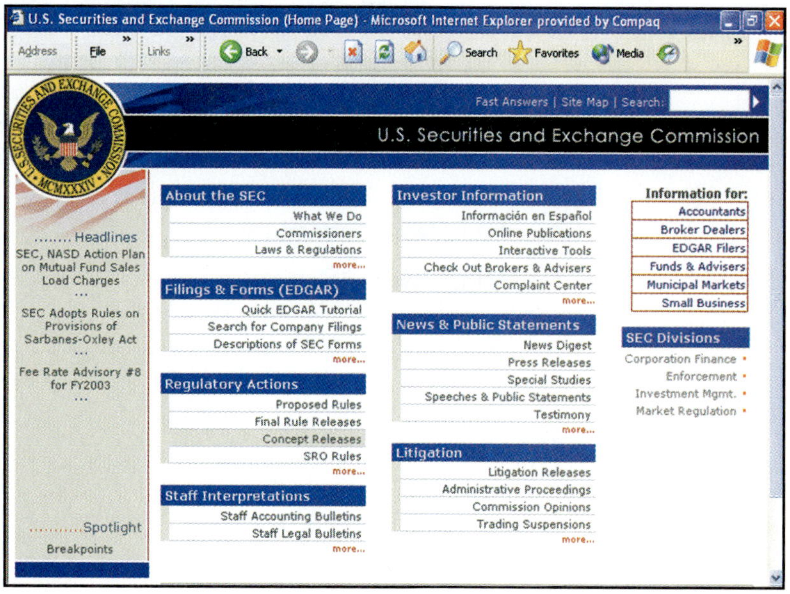

net note

Your login name is used to gain access to a computer and is not necessarily considered private or secret. Your password, on the other hand, is also used to gain access to certain areas, but should be known only to you.

»Stock Price Trends

Internet Address: http:// ____________

____

Description: ____________

____

____

Figure 8.1

Internet Research
challenge:

Ms. Owens has been asked to speak before the Rotary Club. To help her prepare her presentation, she asks you to write a one- to two-page report on the history of the New York Stock Exchange and the impact stock trading has had on the national economy, positively and negatively.

Surf's **up**

http://www.hotmail.com

http://www.trivialpursuit.com

Project #9

THE HUMAN RESOURCES OFFICE

Scenario: This week you are working for Marsha Bayless, human resources manager, at the Romanesque Hotel and Casino in Las Vegas, Nevada. The hotel has over 3,000 employees with a fairly significant turnover rate.

Your Internet tasks for today will focus on a variety of employment issues.

:> TASKS

▶ **9-1**
LOCATE OSHA REPORTING STANDARDS

▶ **9-2**
LOCATE EMPLOYMENT DATA

▶ **9-3**
LOCATE SOCIAL SECURITY RETIREMENT GUIDELINES

▶ **9-4**
DETERMINE ALLOWANCES ON W-4 FORMS

▶ **9-5**
DETERMINE FICA WITHHOLDINGS

LOCATE OSHA REPORTING STANDARDS

An employee, Brent Leigh, was injured in the hotel restaurant. The Occupational Safety and Health Act gives specific guidelines as to the distinction between a recordable injury and a nonrecordable injury. Use the Internet to find and print the explanation of a recordable injury to assist Ms. Bayless in determining whether Mr. Leigh's accident must be reported to the OSHA governing body.

Key Words: **OSHA**

Work Injury Recordkeeping

»EMPLOYMENT ACCIDENTS

Internet Address: http:// _____

Description: _____

Figure 9.1

The Romanesque is an equal employment opportunity company. According to federal EEOC statutes, what characteristics cannot be used as the basis for discrimination in hiring practices?

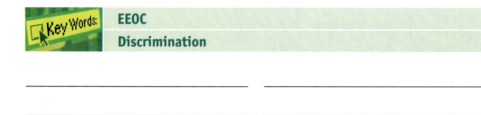

Key Words: EEOC
Discrimination

_____   _____

_____   _____

_____   _____

_____   _____

»EMPLOYMENT DISCRIMINATION

Internet Address: http:// _____

Description: _____

LOCATE SOCIAL SECURITY RETIREMENT GUIDELINES

Marcus Navarro, one of the casino dealers, is approaching his sixty-fifth birthday. He plans to start drawing his social security while continuing to work full time. He wants to know if or how his income will impact his benefits check.

 Key Words: **Social Security Benefits**
Retirement Benefits

_____

_____

_____

_____

_____

»WAGE INFORMATION

Internet Address: http:// _____

Description: _____

Figure 9.2

DETERMINE ALLOWANCES ON W-4 FORMS

All new employees at the Romanesque must complete a W-4 form for federal and state income tax withholding purposes. Ellis Whitney, a new employee, is unsure of how many deduction allowances to list and asks assistance in filling out the form. Using the Internet, find and print a copy of the W-4 form along with its worksheet so he can study his choices before making a decision. Also, can Mr. Whitney elect to have additional tax money withheld from his check on this same form?

Key Words:
IRS
Employment Forms
W-4
Withholding Forms

»EMPLOYMENT FORMS

Internet Address: http:// _____

Description: _____

DETERMINE FICA WITHHOLDINGS

net note

The Internet, originally known as ARPANET, began in 1969 as a project by the U.S. Department of Defense to explore the possibility of a communication network that would be able to survive a nuclear attack.

.COM

Romanesque must withhold FICA (Federal Insurance Contributions Act) tax from all employees' paychecks. This tax is used to fund Social Security and Medicare. Romanesque must also pay matching amounts to the government for these taxes.

What is the percentage each employee must contribute to Social Security, and what is the base wage limit (the maximum taxed earnings) for this tax? What is the percentage each employee must contribute to Medicare?

Key Words:	
	Federal Insurance Contributions Act Tax
	FICA tax
	Social Security Tax
	Withholding Rates

Social Security Rate: _____

Maximum Earnings Taxed: _____

Medicare Rate: _____

»FICA

Internet Address: http:// _____

Description: _____

Internet Research challenge:

The human resources department has noticed an increase in the number of insurance claims dealing with hand injuries among hotel employees. Ms. Bayless plans to address this issue at the next safety meeting in hopes that employees will learn to follow safe practices in their repetitive motion tasks. She would like you to prepare a one- to two-page report describing carpal tunnel syndrome, the causes, the symptoms, and preventive measures employees can adopt to combat this problem.

http://www.livingto100.com

http://www.quicken.com/retirement/planner

Project #10

THE FLEET DEPARTMENT OFFICE

Scenario: You are working as the administrative assistant to J.D. Thomerson, manager of the fleet department of Jenco. Mr. Thomerson needs you to conduct Internet research so he can prepare a report for the company president detailing the cost of purchasing new company vehicles.

Complete the following steps for this Internet task.

Complete the grid below to assist you in gathering information. Employees receive replacement vehicles every three years. The employees who are due for replacement vehicles this year are listed below. To complete the grid, use the current year for the replacement vehicles; subtract three years to fill in the model of vehicles to be replaced. (Example: If the current year is 2003, this would be the New Vehicle Model, and you would use 2000 for the Vehicle to be Replaced.)

net note

You cannot assume that items you find on the Internet are public domain. Most of the material is copyrighted and must be treated accordingly.

New Vehicle Model	Vehicle to Be Replaced	Employee Name
	_____ Honda Accord LX	Stephanie Crisler
	_____ Chrysler Town & Country Van LX	James Anglin
	_____ Ford Taurus LX	Patty Anderson

Figure ≫ 10.1

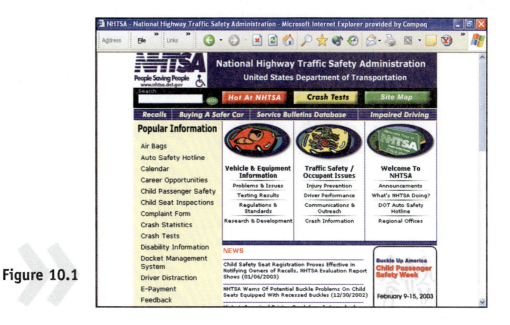

▸ DETERMINE THE CURRENT VALUE OF PRESENT FLEET

You need to determine the current value of the present fleet to use in your final report. Using the Internet, find a site that provides the *trade-in* value of the current vehicles. You can use Kelley Blue Book or NADA prices. All vehicles have power steering, power brakes, power windows, power locks, cassette player, and air bags. The engines are six-cylinder, and the cars are four-door sedans. All vehicles are in good condition. The company vehicles average 12,000 miles a year, so these vehicles have approximately 36,000 miles on them.

Vehicle to Be Replaced (fill in from Task 10-1)	Current Trade-in Value
_____ **Honda Accord LX**	
_____ **Chrysler Town & Country Van LX**	
_____ **Ford Taurus LX**	

Key Words: **Kelley Blue Book**
NADA

»CAR VALUE INFORMATION

Internet Address: http:// _____

Description: _____

LOCATE REPLACEMENT VEHICLES (WITH SAME FEATURES)

You need to determine the cost of the new vehicles. Employees should receive the same vehicle or, if that is not possible, a vehicle that is similar to the one being replaced. Using the Internet, find a site that provides a purchase cost for the new vehicles.

New Vehicle (fill in from Task 10-1)	New Vehicle Cost
_____ Honda Accord LX	
_____ Chrysler Town & Country Van LX	
_____ Ford Taurus LX	

Key Words:	
	New Cars
	Honda
	Chrysler
	Ford

»CAR COST INFORMATION

Internet Address: http:// _____

Description: _____

©2003 NADA Appraisal Guides. Reprinted by permission.

Figure 10.2

TASK 10-4

FIND COST OF PURCHASING VEHICLES AFTER TRADE-IN

You need to determine the total cost if the company decides to purchase the new vehicles. Use the grid below to show your calculations.

New Vehicle (fill in from Task 10-1)	Total Cost of New Vehicle	Less Trade-in Value of Current Fleet Vehicle	Purchase Cost of Vehicle
_____ Honda Accord LX			
_____ Chrysler Town & Country Van LX			
_____ Ford Taurus LX			

CALCULATE TOTAL PAYMENTS AND INTEREST ON NEW CARS

Determine the total cost of the cars by calculating the monthly payments. On the Internet, locate and use a payment calculator. The annual percentage rate is 7.00 percent, and the total number of payments is 36.

net note

The top domains by number of hosts are .com, .edu, and .net

.COM

New Vehicle (fill in from Task 10-1)	Monthly Payment Amount Based on Purchase Price after Trade-In		Total Vehicle Cost (Total of Payments, Including Interest)
_____ Honda Accord LX		× 36	
_____ Chrysler Town & Country Van LX		× 36	
_____ Ford Taurus LX		× 36	

Key Words:
Interest Calculation
Car Payments
Car Loans

»INTEREST CALCULATOR

Internet Address: http:// _____

Description: _____

Internet Research challenge:

In order to determine whether leasing vehicles might be a better option for the company, Mr. Thomerson would like you to research information about leasing vehicles. Prepare a one- to two-page report that explains the advantages and disadvantages of leasing. Examine the sites closely to determine whether they are unbiased resources. Use at least four sources from the Internet to prepare your report. Include information about what types of drivers make good leasing candidates. Mr. Thomerson plans to use this report to prepare for his meeting with his tax adviser next week.

http://www.bigempire.com/vegas/

http://www.emode.com

http://www.dmarie.com/timecap/

Project #11

THE TRAVEL OFFICE

Scenario: Today you are working for the travel department at Lion Oil Company in Dallas, Texas (central time zone). You are responsible for locating and scheduling travel for company executives via the Internet.

Dewana Gober, executive vice president, has a conference to attend in Philadelphia, Pennsylvania. Using the information provided, conduct Internet research, to obtain travel information for Mrs. Gober's trip.

Trip Dates: Departure – One month from today's date
                Return Date – Five days from the departure date (counting departure date as Day 1; for example, leave on January 1; return on January 5)

Travel Details: On the departure date, Mrs. Gober must be in Philadelphia for an 8 p.m. dinner meeting. On her return departure date, Mrs. Gober has a one-hour 8 a.m. meeting. She must be back in time for a dinner engagement at 8 p.m. that evening. *(Note: When making travel arrangements, be sure to allow time for travel to and from the airport – approximately one hour each way – and the required time for check-in at the airport – approximately two hours each way.)*

From the information above, check for available flights that fit Mrs. Gober's travel needs. Mrs. Gober prefers to fly first-class. Compare the round-trip prices from at least two airlines. *(Note: You can go to separate airline sites, but it is easier to use a travel service that checks all airlines at once. There are several free services. Some may require that you sign up for a free membership.)*

Key Words:	American Airlines
	Delta Airlines
	Southwest Airlines
	Northwest Airlines
	Travelocity
	Expedia
	Airtravel
	Preview Travel

Airline #1	Date	Flight #(s)	Departure Time	Arrival Time	Round-trip Fare
					$
Return Trip					
Airline #2	Date	Flight #(s)	Departure Time	Arrival Time	Round-trip Fare
					$
Return Trip					

»AIRLINE SCHEDULING

Internet Address: http:// _____

Description: _____

Figure 11.1

LOCATE HOTEL ACCOMMODATIONS

Mrs. Gober has received recommendations about hotel accommodations from business associates in Philadelphia. Find the standard rate or range of rates for the three Philadelphia hotels listed below so Mrs. Gober can make a final decision on accommodations.

Key Words:
Travelocity
Expedia
Airtravel
Preview Travel
Philadelphia Hotels
Philadelphia On-Line
Hyatt
Marriott

Hotel Name	Standard Room Rate/Range
DoubleTree Hotel	_____
Loews Philadelphia Hotel	_____
Wyndham Franklin Plaza Hotel	_____

»HOTEL ACCOMMODATIONS

Internet Address: http:// _____

Description: _____

DETERMINE BUSINESS TRAVEL EXPENSES

Mrs. Gober has planned another trip the month after her Philadelphia trip, on the 10th of the month. She will be speaking at a conference in Amherst, Massachusetts. She requires only a one-way ticket as she will be starting her vacation after the conference. She has been told that there are no commercial flights into Amherst. Find the least expensive flights to two nearby airports. She will travel by rental car to the conference site. Approximately how many miles will she drive from each airport to Amherst?

Depart on the 10th

Airport #1/ Location _____

Airline _____   Price _____   Rental Miles _____

Airport #2/ Location _____

Airline _____   Price _____   Rental Miles _____

»AIRLINE SCHEDULING:

Internet Address: http:// _____

Description: _____

COMPARE CAR RENTALS

Luis Ramirez, vice president of sales, will be flying into Las Vegas for a meeting with potential clients. His flight was booked last week, but he needs to rent a car. He would like to see a comparison of the various car rental companies and the classes of cars they offer. Using the chart below, provide Mr. Ramirez with information about three car rental companies and prices for renting cars in Las Vegas for one week.

Key Words:	Hertz
	Avis
	Budget
	Travelocity
	Expedia
	Preview Travel

	Car Rental Agency	Car Rental Agency	Car Rental Agency
Class of Car			
Economy	$	$	$
Compact	$	$	$
Mid-Size	$	$	$
Luxury	$	$	$
SUV	$	$	$
Van	$	$	$

»AUTOMOBILE RENTALS

Internet Address: http:// _____

Description: _____

Judi Biss is attending a conference in Houston, Texas. She knows that after her meeting on the 7th, she will need to make copies of the finalized proposal. Your job is to find the address and telephone number for two Kinko's copy centers in the Houston area.

Key Words:	Kinko's
	Yellow Pages

Address/Phone Number: _____

Address/Phone Number: _____

»BUSINESS YELLOW PAGE LISTINGS

Internet Address: http:// _____

Description: _____

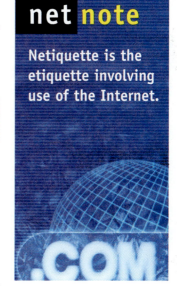

net note

Netiquette is the etiquette involving use of the Internet.

Gary Schepf, from the Buffalo office, is in charge of a business dinner with potential clients in Niagara Falls, Canada. Mr. Schepf wants you to provide him with names and addresses of restaurants in Niagara Falls for this meeting. Using the Internet, find several restaurants you can recommend to Mr. Schepf. He would like you to include the Hard Rock Café in your list.

_____

_____

_____

_____

Internet Research challenge:

It is apparent from the research conducted for this project that airlines charge considerably more for first-class travel. Using sources available on the Internet, such as reports and individual airline sites, prepare a one- to two-page report describing the amenities offered in first class by various airlines.

http://www.orbitz.com

http://www.cnn.com/TRAVEL/

http://www.hshawaii.com

Project #12

THE PURCHASING OFFICE

Scenario: This week you are working for Diego Fuentes in the purchasing office of Summerfield Trophies. The company has recently expanded and is getting ready to relocate its offices to a new building. The purchasing office is in the process of gathering pricing information and specifications on new office furniture and equipment. You have been hired to provide the Internet research necessary to help make these purchasing decisions.

TASK 12-1

LOCATE OFFICE PLANNING SERVICES AND PRODUCTS

Donnie McGahee, president of Summerfield Trophies, has requested information about office cubicles. The new building has a large room that needs to be subdivided. He would like the name of a company that can help plan the space and provide layout suggestions for the office.

 **Key Words:** **Office Cubicles**
Office Layout Planning

Company Name: _____

Web Site Address: _____

»OFFICE LAYOUTS AND CUBICLES

Internet Address: http:// _____

Description: _____

TASK 12-2

LOCATE AND COMPARE PAPER SHREDDERS

The records manager, Dick Uhler, has requested that you do some comparison shopping and pricing for office shredders. Though the business does not have large quantities of security-sensitive materials, it does need to dispose of certain business, employee, and customer information in a secure manner. Mr. Uhler would like to know the difference between a straight-cut and cross-cut shredder. He would also like you to recommend a price and model for a straight-cut and cross-cut shredder that can process up to 100 sheets per day.

 Key Words: **Shredder Comparison**
Shredder Pricing

Description:

Straight-Cut Shredder: _____

_____

_____

Cross-Cut Shredder: _____

_____

_____

Recommendation (based on up to 100 sheets per day):

Straight-Cut Shredder

Model: _____

Price: _____

Cross-Cut Shredder

Model: _____

Price: _____

»PAPER SHREDDERS

Internet Address: http:// _____

Description: _____

▶ LOCATE NAME TAG SOURCE

Carolyn Cox, the store manager, wants all employees to wear company name tags while on the job. She asks you to find a source for ordering name tags that can be customized with a one-color company logo and two lines of text (employee name and position). She would like to have magnetic backs on the name tags rather than the traditional pin. In the space provided, supply the name of the company, its web site address, and the total price for 50 name tags (including handling and any setup fee for a logo).

 Key Words: **Magnetic Name Tags**
Employee Name Tags

_____

_____

_____

»NAME TAGS

Internet Address: http:// _____

Description: _____

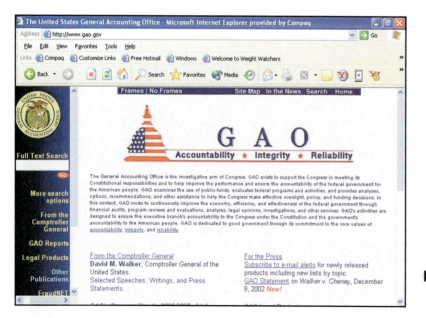

Figure 12.1

COMPARE PRICES OF COMMON OFFICE SUPPLIES

Rachel Underwood, the office manager, has sent a request for some common office supplies. Mr. Fuentes likes to check out the various sources of office supplies periodically to determine if there is any significant difference in the price of items purchased. After filling Ms. Underwood's order, you are to compare three of those items at various online sources. Be sure to use identical or near identical items for your comparisons.

Supplies Requisition

Date: _____ 11/01 _____   Date Needed: _____ 11/07 _____

Requested by _____ Rachel Underwood _____

Authorized by: _____ Shadrack Sietsa _____

Qty.	Item
6	3 x 3 Sticky Note Pads
12	#2 Pencils
1 box	100 #1 smooth paper clips
1 roll	1" invisible tape
3	Yellow legal pads
1	Tape dispenser for 1" tape
1 ream	Copy paper — white, standard weight and brightness

Using the chart below, check out prices at three major online suppliers (i.e., Office Max, Office Depot, Staples, and Viking). Indicate the supplier name, items compared, and prices.

	Supplier:	Supplier:	Supplier:
Item:			
Item:			
Item:			

»Office Supplies

Internet Address: http:// _____

Description: _____

RESEARCH GOLD INFORMATION

Gold plating is often used on the finer awards produced by Summerfield Trophies. Randy McElvey, the chief designer, has requested that you use the Internet to determine today's New York spot price for one ounce of gold. Pure gold is generally too soft for most applications, so it must be alloyed with other metals for strength. What is the lowest karat designation that can still be classified as gold in the United States, and how much of that metal is actually gold?

Key Words: **Gold Price**
Karat System

Gold price per ounce: _____

Minimum karat designation: _____ Percentage of gold _____

»Gold Information

Internet Address: http:// _____

Description: _____

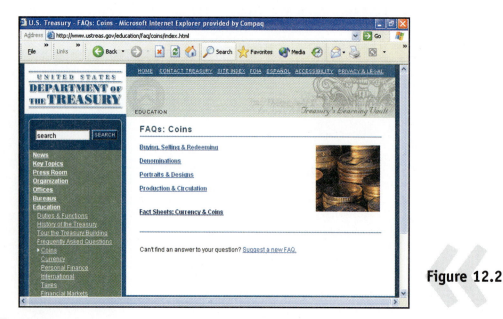

Figure 12.2

Internet Research challenge:

In designing the new office space, Mr. McGahee has asked you to research the various effects of color in an environment. Prepare a one- to two-page report describing the research findings of how color affects mood and productivity of office workers.

http://home.att.net/~cecw/lastpage.htm

http://www.phonespell.org/

Project #13

THE CREDIT OFFICE

Scenario: Today you are working for Pat Jeter, store manager, in the credit office of a large department store that offers its own credit cards to customers. Finance charges to credit customers are a significant source of income for corporations today. Your Internet assignments will help in the formulation of credit policies and practices.

Credit offices must keep track of a number of interest rates in order to establish their own competetive rate. One of the most fundamental interest rates in the nation is the fed funds rate set by the Federal Open Market Committee. Determine the

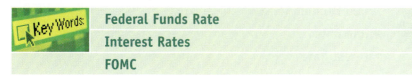

Key Words:	**Federal Funds Rate**
	Interest Rates
	FOMC

Federal Funds Target Rate: _____

»FEDERAL FUNDS "TARGET" RATE

Internet Address: http:// _____

Description: _____

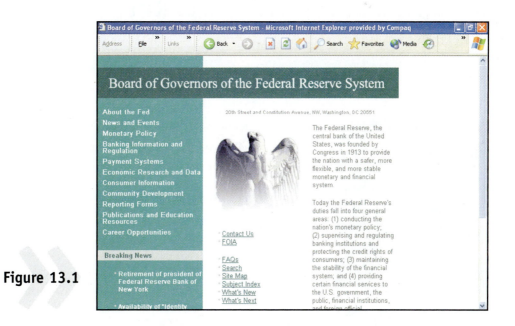

Figure 13.1

DETERMINE THE PRIME LENDING RATE

Another interest rate used to help establish credit card charge rates is the prime lending rate. Use the Internet to determine the current prime rate. The credit manager, Gloria Montes, likes to keep things in perspective. In addition to the current prime rate, she would like you to find out what the prime rate was exactly 20 years ago today.

Key Words:	Prime Lending Rate
	Prime Rate
	Interest Rate

Current Prime Rate: _____

Prime Rate 20 years ago: _____

»PRIME RATE

Internet Address: http:// _____

Description: _____

DETERMINE U.S. PERSONAL SAVINGS RATE

net note

Google, Yahoo, MSN, and AOL combined accounted for almost 93 percent of all global search referrals to shopping web sites on December 1, 2002.

Credit card purchases are a form of borrowing; eventually they must be paid out of current income or savings. Find and print a chart showing the U.S. personal savings rate over the past several decades.

During what decade was the savings rate the highest?

_____

| Key Words: | Personal Savings Rate |
| | U.S. Savings Rate |

»PERSONAL SAVINGS

Internet Address: http:// _____

Description: _____

LOCATE CREDIT CARD INTEREST RATES

Dale Rice, chief financial officer, is always concerned with what interest rates other credit cards are charging. For his information, list three bank-issued MasterCards and their APR (annual percentage rate) charges.

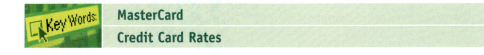

| Key Words: | MasterCard |
| | Credit Card Rates |

MasterCard   Interest Rate

_____   _____

_____   _____

_____   _____

»CREDIT CARD INTEREST RATES

Internet Addresses: http:// _____

Description: _____

TASK 13-5

LOCATE CREDIT BUREAUS

Not everyone who wants a credit card is creditworthy. List three major credit bureaus that do credit searches on potential customers.

Key Words: **Credit Bureaus**
Credit Searches

Major Credit Bureaus

_____

_____

_____

»MAJOR CREDIT BUREAUS

Internet Address: http:// _____

Description: _____

Figure 13.2

Internet Research **challenge:**

Today individuals and companies face a growing problem of credit fraud caused by identity theft. Write a one- to two-page report detailing the extent of the problem and steps that can be taken by both the individual and the company to prevent future occurrences.

Surf's **up**

http://tv.yahoo.com

http://www.shockwave.com/sw/content/bullyproof

Project #14

MOVING AND LIVING INDEPENDENTLY

Scenario: Your job search and work experience have paid off! You receive attractive job offers from four companies. Now you just have to make the decision as to whose job to accept and where your new home will be. There are many considerations to look at when making such a big decision.

You received four job offers. Now you want to compare the offers to determine which is best. The site listed below can be used to do cost-of-living comparisons, after which you will indicate the job you would choose based solely on a salary comparison. You currently live in Nacogdoches, Texas, and have been offered a job there at a salary of $30,000.

http://www.homefair.com — Choose "The Salary Calculator."

Using the chart below, provide the salary equivalents for each of the job offer locations. In the Dollar Amount column, indicate the amount needed in the new city to be equivalent to $30,000 in Nacogdoches. In the Plus or Minus column, include the difference between the actual offer and the equivalent of the Nacogdoches offer. Use the "own" option for determining the costs.

Nacogdoches, Texas, annual salary of $30,000 is equal to . . .			
Dollar Amount	City	Offer	Plus or Minus
	Valdosta, GA	$38,000	
	San Diego, CA	$40,000	
	New York (Manhattan), NY	$85,000	

Based on a salary comparison, your job choice would be _____ .

RESEARCH CRIME OCCURRENCES

Living in a safe environment is also a consideration for moving to a new location. Using the Relocation Crime Lab link at the Homefair web site, complete the chart below, providing the current crime rate for each of the locations under consideration.

Nacogdoches, Texas	
Valdosta, Georgia	
San Diego, California	
New York (Manhattan), New York	

Which is the safest place to live? _____

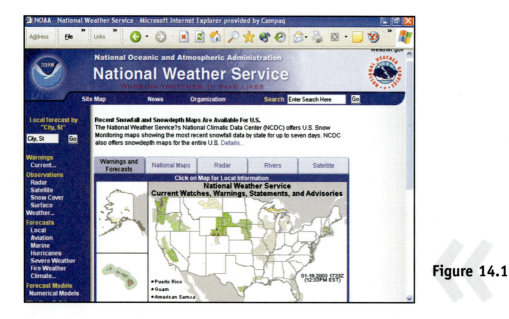

Figure 14.1

Using the "City Reports" link at the Homefair web site, fill in the chart below for a quick comparison of the various cities in which you have been offered a job.

Population	Nacogdoches, Texas	
	Valdosta, Georgia	
	San Diego, California	
	New York (Manhattan), New York	
Annual Snowfall	Nacogdoches, Texas	
	Valdosta, Georgia	
	San Diego, California	
	New York (Manhattan), New York	
Annual Rainfall	Nacogdoches, Texas	
	Valdosta, Georgia	
	San Diego, California	
	New York (Manhattan), New York	
Sales Tax (State and Local)	Nacogdoches, Texas	
	Valdosta, Georgia	
	San Diego, California	
	New York (Manhattan), New York	
Property Tax Rate	Nacogdoches, Texas	
	Valdosta, Georgia	
	San Diego, California	
	New York (Manhattan), New York	
Price of a 3-Bedroom House	Nacogdoches, Texas	
	Valdosta, Georgia	
	San Diego, California	
	New York (Manhattan), New York	
Rent for a 2-Bedroom Apartment	Nacogdoches, Texas	
	Valdosta, Georgia	
	San Diego, California	
	New York (Manhattan), New York	

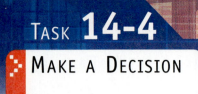

Now that you have gathered information about all of the job locations, in the space provided, give your decision as to the location you have chosen and your rationale for choosing it.

Your location choice: _____

Your rationale:

_____

_____

_____

_____

_____

_____

_____

_____

_____

_____

Figure 14.2

Using the Internet, find and list sites you can use to locate rentals or properties for sale in the proposed job locations.

Nacogdoches, Texas	
Valdosta, Georgia	
San Diego, California	
New York (Manhattan), New York	

Internet Research challenge:

Finding a new home in a new town is a major undertaking. Write a one- to two-page report providing the advantages and disadvantages of renting versus owning a home. Include such things as investment considerations, tax implications, income tax deductions, and home office possibilities.

Surf's up

Dilbert Zone – **http://www.unitedmedia.com/comics/dilbert**

ESPN – **http://msn.espn.go.com/main.html**

Project #15

PLANNING A VACATION

Scenario: Now that you have worked a full year at your new job, you have earned a well-deserved week of vacation. Use the Internet to research information necessary for an exciting trip to London!

OBTAIN A PASSPORT

net note

Looking at the URL following the dot can tell you something about the site you are visiting. Common types of sites include: .com (commercial), .edu (educational), .gov (governmental), .mil (military), .net (network provider), and .org (organizational).

You have never had a passport before. Which passport application form must you fill out? _____

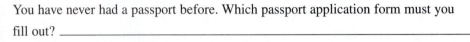

Key Words:
Passport
U.S. State Department
United States Post Office

Provide the necessary address for mailing in your passport application.

_____

Unfortunately, you cannot find your birth certificate for the passport application. How can you get a certified copy of your birth certificate? Provide the necessary address.

_____

_____

_____

How much is the regular cost for a ten-year passport? _____

»PASSPORT INFORMATION

Internet Address: http:// _____

_____

_____

Description: _____

_____

_____

Figure 15.1

If you get in trouble overseas, you need to know how to contact the American Embassy. Locate the address and telephone number for the embassy.

 American Embassy in London

London Tourist Information

US Information Agency

Provide the address and phone number for the American Embassy in London.

_____

_____

»EMBASSY INFORMATION

Internet Address: http:// _____

Description: _____

net note

In addition to being able to tell the type of site from looking at the URL, you can often also tell the country; for example, au (Australia); ca (Canada); es (Spain); fr (France); uk (United Kingdom); and us (United States).

.COM

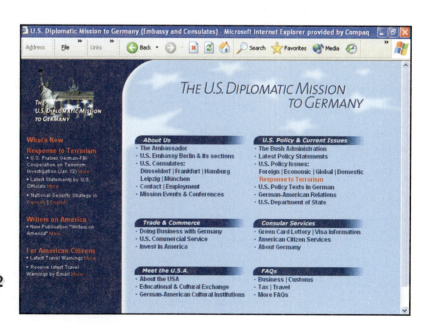

Figure 15.2

TASK 15-3

LOCATE PUBLIC TRANSPORTATION

While in London, you may want to utilize the world-famous London Underground (subway). Find and print a copy of this system's map.

London Underground Map

London

»PUBLIC TRANSPORTATION INFORMATION

Internet Address: http:// _____

Description: _____

TASK 15-4

LOCATE ACCOMMODATIONS

If you are interested in history, you may want to stay near the Tower of London. Find the names, addresses, and prices of two hotels in this historic area.

London Hotels

Hotel 1   Name: _____

Address: _____

Price: _____

Hotel 2   Name: _____

Address: _____

Price: _____

»ACCOMMODATIONS IN LONDON

Internet Address: http:// _____

Description: _____

RESEARCH SIGHTSEEING ATTRACTIONS

Two of the most famous attractions in London are Buckingham Palace and Tower Bridge. What time does the Changing of the Guard take place at the Palace? On average, how many cars travel across the bridge each day?

London Sightseeing

Sightseeing in London

London Attractions

Time of Changing of the Guard: _____

Daily Traffic across Tower Bridge: _____

»LONDON ATTRACTIONS

Internet Address: http:// _____

Description: _____

EXCHANGE FOREIGN CURRENCY

You will need some local cash even if you plan to charge most of your expenses using a credit card. If you change 500 American dollars into British pounds, how many pounds will you receive? _____

At the end of your vacation, you have 83 pounds left. How much will you receive when this money is converted back to American dollars? _____

Currency Exchange

Foreign Exchange Rates

»CURRENCY EXCHANGE RATES

Internet Address: http:// _____

Description: _____

net note

When verbally reciting a URL, the . in the address is called a dot — not a period.

Internet Research challenge:

One of the most famous and beautiful buildings in London is St. Paul's Cathedral. Use Internet sources to prepare a one- to two-page report detailing its history and architecture. Include information that explains why one area is named the Whispering Gallery.

Surf's up

http://www.frommers.com

http://www.wtgonline.com

http://www.atevo.com

Project #16

WEB PAGE DESIGN

Scenario: You have been asked to create your own web page for a class assignment. You have a short amount of time in which to complete the project. Your colleagues have advised you that the simplest web page can be created using HyperText Markup Language (HTML). They have told you about online HTML tutorials that can help you create a web page. You have found the following online HTML tutorial to be helpful: *http://www.davesite. com/webstation/html.*

The following tasks will assist you in beginning your class assignment.

TASK 16-1

IDENTIFY TAGS IN HYPERTEXT MARKUP LANGUAGE

net note

HTML, the acronym for HyperText Markup Language, is used to create web pages. HTML is not difficult to learn or to master. You can compose HTML text on any word processor or with an HTML editor.

Define what *tags* are in HTML. Be descriptive in your definition.

_____

_____

_____

_____

_____

_____

_____

TASK 16-2

DEFINE TAGS

Define the four main tags in HTML. What tag identifies the beginning of an HTML document?

_____

_____

_____

_____

_____

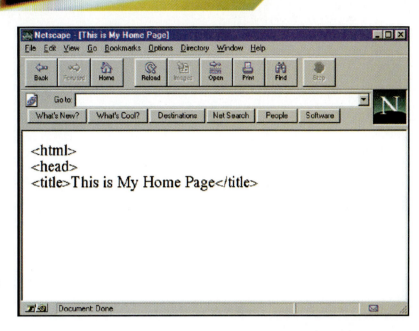

Figure 16.1

What are the six levels of headings? Give an example of each type of heading.

_____

_____

_____

_____

_____

_____

_____

_____

net note

When saving your HTML document, you must use the extension .htm. This indicates to a web browser that the document has HTML-coded information.

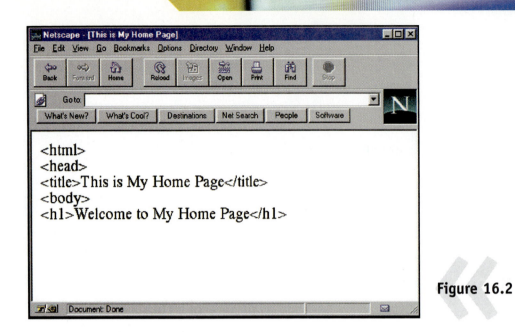

```
<html>
<head>
<title>This is My Home Page</title>
<body>
<h1>Welcome to My Home Page</h1>
```

Figure 16.2

HTML PARAGRAPHS

How are paragraphs recognized in HTML?

_____

_____

_____

_____

_____

_____

_____

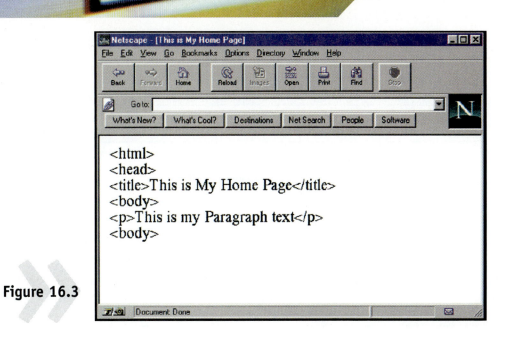

```
<html>
<head>
<title>This is My Home Page</title>
<body>
<p>This is my Paragraph text</p>
<body>
```

Figure 16.3

HTML-REQUIRED ELEMENTS

What are the required elements for a simple HTML document? Describe why these elements are necessary.

_____

_____

_____

_____

_____

_____

_____

_____

Figure 16.4

DESIGN A WEB PAGE

Based on your responses in the previous tasks, create a simple HTML document. The document should contain the following:

• Title tag

• Document heading

• One paragraph with a body of text

Extra credit:

• One graphic

• An off-site link

You can use any HTML editor to create your web page, or you can download a free HTML editor at the following web site:

http://www.brooknorth.com (follow the Download Free 30 Day Trial! link)

You may use any of the online tutorials (See **Surf's Up**) for this task. Submit the following for grading:

• Printout of HTML source code

• Floppy disk containing completed web page in presentation view

Internet Research challenge:

Carefully study the design and format of each of the following web sites:

- http://stars.com (sensory)
- http://www.sun.com (conceptual)
- http://developer.netscape.com (reactive)

Discuss the design elements you found to be most effective, and make suggestions for improvement. Does the site employ any new, cutting-edge technology? If so, describe it.

_____

_____

_____

_____

Surf's up

http://www.cs.cmu.edu/People/tilt/cgh/

http://www.w3.org/MarkUp/MarkUp.html

http://www.ucc.ie/info/net/htmldoc.html

http://www.werbach.com/barebones/

Additional reading:
Castro, Elizabeth. _HTML for the World Wide Web_. Berkeley: Peachpit, 1997